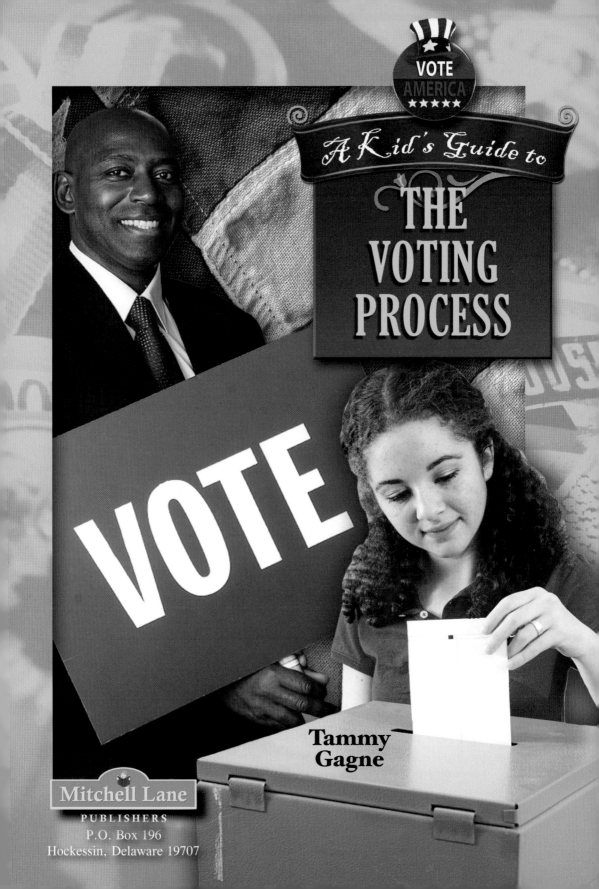

VOTE
AMERICA
★★★★★

A Kid's Guide to

THE VOTING PROCESS

VOTE

Tammy
Gagne

Mitchell Lane
PUBLISHERS
P.O. Box 196
Hockessin, Delaware 19707

A History of the Democratic Party
A History of the Republican Party
A History of Voting Rights
A Kid's Guide to the Voting Process

Printing   2   3   4   5   6   7   8   9

Library of Congress Cataloging-in-Publication Data

Gagne, Tammy.
 A kid's guide to the voting process / by Tammy Gagne.
    p. cm. — (Vote America)
 Includes bibliographical references and index.
 ISBN 978-1-61228-260-2 (library bound)
 1. Voting—United States—Juvenile literature.
 I. Title.
 JK1978.G34 2012
 324.60973—dc23
                                              2012007538

eBook ISBN: 9781612283364

                                              PLB

CONTENTS

Chapter One
The Right to Vote 4

Chapter Two
The Life of the Party 12

Chapter Three
Does Every Vote Make a Difference? 22

Chapter Four
Close to Home 28

Chapter Five
What You Can Do for Your Country 34

Timeline 42
Chapter Notes 43
Further Reading
Books 44
Works Consulted 44
On the Internet 45

Glossary 46

Index 47

The Right to Vote

Night had just fallen on Griffin's Wharf on December 16, 1773. At first glance, the American colonists looked like Native Americans. Many had disguised themselves in feather headdresses and leather hides. They didn't want anyone to know who they were as they stood on the decks of three different ships in Boston Harbor. The *Beaver, Dartmouth,* and *Eleanor* had brought tea to the colonies from China.

British merchants planned to sell this tea to the colonists, and King George III planned to charge them taxes on it. The colonists believed these taxes were unfair, and they had planned to destroy the tea in protest. They wanted to show the king and the British government how they felt about these unfair taxes. The colonists ended up dumping 342 chests of tea—more than 46 tons—into the Atlantic Ocean.[1] The entire harbor smelled like tea, but what was truly brewing was a war.

Some people think it is odd that we accept taxes so easily today after our ancestors fought so hard against them. Taxes are now part of everyday life in the United States. We pay taxes on our income, our property, and yes, sometimes even our tea. There is

The Boston Tea Party was an organized protest to gain American colonists the right to vote.

one big difference between the taxes we pay today, however, and the taxes that the American colonists had to pay to England. As American citizens, we have a say in the process. The colonists did not. They were not allowed to be part of the government that made decisions about taxes and all other laws they had to follow. This issue turned into one of the biggest slogans of the American Revolution: *No taxation without representation!*

In 1783, the American colonists won the Revolutionary War against England. At this time the country's founding fathers decided that the new nation would not have a king as Great Britain did. The United States of America would be a democracy. The basic idea of democracy is that each person has a vote. Decisions are made by the biggest group of people who agree. That is not the end of the story, though.

Not every person in the United States could vote at first. The U.S. Constitution was ratified in 1788. It gave white men who were at least 21 years of age and owned a certain amount of land the right to vote. Some states also had voting restrictions. Maryland, North Carolina, and South Carolina required men to own at least 50 acres of land to receive voting rights. If a South Carolina man wanted to run for a public office, he needed to own ten times this amount of land—at least 500 acres.

Landowners, also called freeholders, were thought to care about the community more than men who owned no land. Voting was seen less as a right and more as a privilege that went with land ownership. Men who did not own land were denied the right to vote. Lawmakers believed that these men would simply vote the way their landowners wanted them to.

The colonists felt strongly that if they had to pay taxes to the king of England, they should have a say in British government. When the United States broke away from Great Britain, people still believed in the slogan from the war—no taxation without representation. However, the phrase was being taken quite literally. Since only freeholders paid taxes, men who did not own property were not represented by anyone in the government.

"Today a man owns a jackass worth fifty dollars, and he is entitled to vote; but before the next election the jackass dies. The man in the meantime has become more experienced . . . and he is therefore better qualified to make a proper selection of rulers. But the jackass is dead, and the man cannot vote. Now, gentlemen, pray inform me, in whom is the right of suffrage? In the man or in the jackass?"—Benjamin Franklin

Land ownership was not the only requirement for full voting rights at this time. Several states would not allow Jews, Roman Catholics, or atheists to serve in the government. This situation angered many people. Men who had risked their lives for the nation's independence could neither vote nor hold public office in it. Men of color and women were also denied voting rights.

THIS IS THE ONLY PLANTATION IN THE NATION THAT HAS TAXATION WITHOUT REPRESENTATION

Founded on July 16, 1790, Washington, D.C., is not officially a state. According to the U.S. Constitution, then, its residents do not have representation in Congress. They could not vote for president, either, until 1961, when the Twenty-third Amendment was passed.

Some of the country's founding fathers—and mothers—worked for suffrage, or voting rights for everyone. One of the leading suffragists was Benjamin Franklin. He thought it was both foolish and unfair to base voting rights on property ownership or religious beliefs. After all, didn't the earliest settlers of America come to these shores in part to gain religious freedom? By 1830, most states had abolished voting restrictions based on land ownership or religion.

Suffragists were still working toward changing laws to make voting a right for everyone, though. In 1848, the first women's rights convention took place in Seneca Falls, New York. Two of the women behind this event were Susan B. Anthony and Elizabeth Cady Stanton, both suffrage activists. More than 300 people attended the convention, including 40 men.

Anthony and Stanton had different lifestyles and strengths to bring to the movement. Anthony was unmarried. She spent most of her time making speeches about the importance of women's rights. Stanton was married and had several children. She used her writing skills to do her part for the cause. Together they created the National Woman Suffrage Association.[2] Still, it would be many years before women won the right to vote.

In the meantime, the Civil War was looming. Most people from the Northern states thought slavery was wrong. They thought all men and women should be free. Most of the people in the Southern states who owned slaves wanted to be able to keep them. They wanted life to continue the way it had for generations. The Northern states won the Civil War in 1865, but it was still five more years before the Fifteenth Amendment granted African-American men the right to vote. Some states tried to work around

By 1860, only five states had granted African Americans the same voting rights that white men possessed. These states were Maine, Massachusetts, New Hampshire, Vermont, and Rhode Island.

Elizabeth Cady Stanton and Susan B. Anthony helped women get the right to vote.

this new law. Some charged poll taxes. Others made voters take literacy tests prior to voting. Since many African Americans were poor and could not read, they were still being denied the right to vote.

People who supported the women's suffrage movement continued their fight during this time. In 1872, thirteen women joined Susan B. Anthony in voting in an election in Rochester, New York. They were all arrested a few days later, but their bold move got the attention of people both near and far. More and more states began upholding women's right to vote. In 1920, the Nineteenth Amendment granted all women the right to vote.

 Women fought hard to receive the same voting rights that men had. The women marching in this New York City parade in 1912 would have to wait eight more years before the Nineteenth Amendment would be added to the Constitution.

African Americans and women had made enormous progress, and with the 1924 Indian Citizenship Act, Native American citizens were able to follow suit. Nonetheless, voting discrimination was far from over. Everyone had the right to vote, but it wasn't being honored in many Southern states. The 1960s were a time of great political change. This decade is often called the civil rights era for this reason. People were speaking up and demanding to be heard about the importance of equal treatment for everyone. In 1964, the Twenty-fourth Amendment did away with poll taxes. This move was followed up by the Voting Rights Act of 1965, which made literacy tests for voting illegal as well.[3]

The Fifteenth Amendment gave African Americans the right to vote, but many states used poll taxes and literacy tests to keep them from doing so. Finally, in the 1960s, both schemes were made illegal.

Chapter 2

The Life of the Party

On April 28, 2009, Senator Arlen Specter of Pennsylvania made a surprising announcement. After 29 years as a Republican senator, he decided to become a Democrat. "I now find my political philosophy more in line with Democrats than Republicans," he explained in his official statement about the decision. But what caused him to make this move? What had changed?

He told reporters that he thought Republicans were becoming too extreme in their views. He didn't think many Republicans were willing to work with Democrats to accomplish important goals. He said he wanted to vote for what he thought was right. He said he didn't want to vote with the other members of his party just for the sake of remaining loyal to them.[1]

Some people thought Senator Specter's reasons had more to do with his own success. More than 200,000 Republican voters in his state had re-registered as Democrats over the previous year. Specter hadn't been doing well in his race against the other Republicans. Perhaps he thought that changing his party along with them would give him a greater chance of keeping his seat in the Senate.

When Senator Arlen Specter changed parties from Republican to Democratic in 2009, it wasn't the first time he had switched. He was a registered Democrat until he switched to the Republican Party in the mid-1960s.

No one can say for sure whether Senator Specter had his state's and country's best interests or his own in mind when he decided to switch parties. He wasn't able to save his seat with the move, though. He lost the Democratic primary election to Joe Sestak. Pat Toomey, the Republican candidate, won the race in November 2010.

Ready, Register, Vote!

Today every citizen of the United States who is at least 18 years of age has the right to vote. This right may be taken away, however, if a person commits a serious crime. All convicted felons lose their voting rights during their time in jail. Some states restore these rights when the felon is released, but many do not.

Each citizen cannot vote on every issue that needs to be decided. Doing so would take too much time and cost too much money. For this reason we elect representatives, including senators, governors, and mayors. We each vote for the person whose views best match our own. These people take the time to review and research different issues before they vote on them.

Before anyone can vote in an election, he or she must register. Some states allow young people to register to vote while they are still 17 if they will turn 18 by the next election.[2] Registering is fast, simple, and free. Voter registration is important because it ensures that each person votes only once. New voters can register at their local motor vehicles office, social services agency, or city hall. Some states require in-person registration. Some allow people to register online. In either case, all new voters must provide identification and proof of where they live.

In addition to making sure that no one votes more than once, registration also helps the government prepare for the voting process. Each state must have the right number of ballots or voting machines on hand at each poll before Election Day. Having too many forms or computers is a waste, especially if another area has too few. Each poll also needs a certain number of volunteers

Texas Voter Registration Application

Prescribed by the Office of the Secretary of State   VR17.2011E.13

For Official Use Only

Please complete sections by printing LEGIBLY. If you have any questions about how to fill out this application, please call your local voter registrar.

1 These Questions Must Be Completed Before Proceeding

Check one

☐ New Application   ☐ Change of Address, Name, or Other Information   ☐ Request for a Replacement Card

Are you a United States Citizen?   ☐ Yes   ☐ No

Will you be 18 years of age on or before election day?   ☐ Yes   ☐ No

If you checked 'No' in response to either of the above, do not complete this form.

Are you interested in serving as an election worker?   ☐ Yes   ☐ No

2 **Last Name** Include Suffix if any (Jr, Sr, III)   **First Name**   **Middle Name** (If any)   **Former Name** (if any)

3 **Residence Address:** Street Address and Apartment Number. If none, describe where you live. (Do not include P.O. Box, Rural Rt. or Business Address)   **City**   **TEXAS**   **County**   **Zip Code**

4 **Mailing Address:** Street Address and Apartment Number. (If mail cannot be delivered to your residence address.)   **City**   **State**   **Zip Code**

5 **Date of Birth:** (mm/dd/yyyy) ☐☐/☐☐/☐☐☐☐

6 **Gender** (Optional)   ☐ Male   ☐ Female

7 **Telephone Number** (Optional) Include Area Code   (☐☐☐)☐☐☐-☐☐☐☐

8 **Texas Driver's License No. or Texas Personal I.D. No.** (Issued by the Department of Public Safety)   ☐☐☐☐☐☐☐☐

If no Texas Driver's License or Personal Identification, give last 4 digits of your Social Security Number   XXX-XX-☐☐☐☐

☐ I have not been issued a Texas Driver's License/Personal Identification Number or Social Security Number.

9 I understand that giving false information to procure a voter registration is perjury, and a crime under state and federal law. Conviction of this crime may result in imprisonment up to 180 days, a fine up to $2,000, or both. Please read all <u>three</u> statements to affirm before signing.

- I am a resident of this county and a U.S. citizen;
- I have not been finally convicted of a felony, or if a felon, I have completed all of my punishment including any term of incarceration, parole, supervision, period of probation, or I have been pardoned; and
- I have not been determined by a final judgment of a court exercising probate jurisdiction to be totally mentally incapacitated or partially mentally incapacitated without the right to vote.

X _____   Date ___ / ___ / ___

Signature of Applicant or Agent and Relationship to Applicant or Printed Name of Applicant if Signed by Witness and Date.

A sample of a Texas voter registration application. In order to vote, all citizens must fill out a voter registration form.

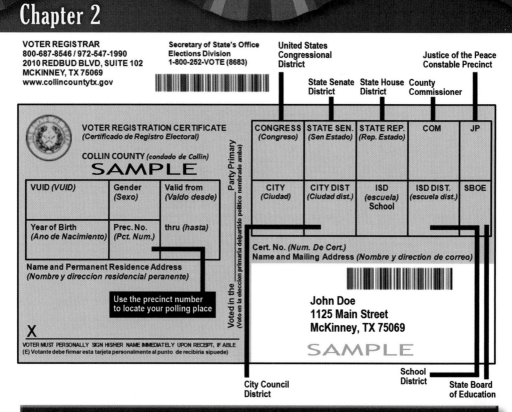

VOTER REGISTRAR
800-687-8546 / 972-547-1990
2010 REDBUD BLVD, SUITE 102
MCKINNEY, TX 75069
www.collincountytx.gov

Secretary of State's Office
Elections Division
1-800-252-VOTE (8683)

United States
Congressional
District

Justice of the Peace
Constable Precinct

State Senate State House County
District   District   Commissioner

VOTER REGISTRATION CERTIFICATE
(Certificado de Registro Electoral)

COLLIN COUNTY *(condado de Collin)*

SAMPLE

Party Primary
(partido politico departido primaria eleccion en la ambla)

CONGRESS *(Congreso)*	STATE SEN. *(Sen Estado)*	STATE REP. *(Rep. Estado)*	COM	JP

VUID *(VUID)*	Gender *(Sexo)*	Valid from *(Valdo desde)*

CITY *(Ciudad)*	CITY DIST. *(Ciudad dist.)*	ISD *(escuela)* School	ISD DIST. *(escuela dist.)*	SBOE

Year of Birth *(Ano de Nacimiento)*	Prec. No. *(Pct. Num.)*	thru *(hasta)*

Name and Permanent Residence Address
(Nombre y direccion residencial peranente)

Use the precinct number
to locate your polling place

X

VOTER MUST PERSONALLY SIGN HIS/HER NAME IMMEDIATELY UPON RECEIPT, IF ABLE
(E) Votante debe firmar esta tarjeta personalmente al punto de recibiria sipuede)

Voted in the
(Voto en la eleccion primaria departido politico nombrado ambla)

Cert. No. *(Num. De Cert.)*
Name and Mailing Address *(Nombre y direccion de correo)*

John Doe
1125 Main Street
McKinney, TX 75069

SAMPLE

City Council
District

School
District

State Board
of Education

Some states provide voters with voter registration cards prior to Election Day. The voters use these cards as identification at the polls. Some states also require voters to show a photo ID, such as a driver's license.

to verify voters' names, hand out the ballots, and make sure that all the marked ballots are collected properly.

Each person's vote is confidential. Voters are not required to tell anyone how they voted, but they may choose to share this information. A curtain usually hangs in front of the entrance to each voting booth for privacy. There is usually room for only one person per booth, though children are often allowed to go into the booth with a parent. Volunteers sometimes give people stickers that say "I voted today" when they leave.

When voters go to the polls, they can usually meet a few of the local candidates running for office. Candidates typically shake voters' hands and ask for their votes that day. They also answer any questions the voters may have for them. Everyone will smile and act politely, but oftentimes the candidates standing side by side are running against each other. These opponents belong to different political parties.

Political parties are groups made up of people who share many opinions. Belonging to a party helps candidates get elected, since the party helps raise campaign funds for its members. A candidate can also receive help from volunteers who belong to the same party. Even politicians who have already been elected participate in this process. The president of the United States often spends time stumping for local candidates who belong to his party. Like- wise a state's senators may endorse a candidate running for mayor in his or her area.

The United States has two main political parties: the Demo- cratic Party and the Republican Party. Members of each party usually have common views on key issues. These views have evolved over the years. Today, Democrats believe that many prob- lems can be solved by creating new laws. Many Republicans believe in gradual change and smaller government. Just as people can vote for whomever they choose, candidates can belong to one party and share certain views with another. A person whose views aren't extreme in either direction is called a moderate. Both Democrats and Republicans can be moderates.

Party members often vote together on issues to help accom- plish the goals of the group. For instance, Democrats generally believe in stricter gun control laws, while Republicans do not. The Second Amendment of the U.S. Constitution grants Americans the right to bear arms. Democrats and Republicans disagree about

The term *stumping* means "making speeches to voters." In the early years of our nation, many candidates would stand on the highest nearby object—often an actual tree stump—to address the people.

exactly what the founding fathers intended when they wrote this part of the document. Republicans usually oppose laws that restrict this freedom in any way. The chances of passing a new gun control law are greater when there are more Democrats in Congress. When the ratio of Democrats to Republicans is close, moderates often hold the deciding votes.

When Americans register to vote, they may register as a Democrat, a Republican, or an Independent. Likewise, each candidate is registered as one of these three. An unlimited number of people can run for president, for example, but only one person receives the nomination of his or her party.

Many voters choose to register as independents. They prefer not to label themselves as either Democrat or Republican. The only disadvantage to registering as an independent is that inde-

The donkey symbolizes the Democratic party.

The elephant symbolizes the Republican party.

pendents are not always allowed to vote in primary elections. In a primary election, voters choose one candidate from their party. In most states, registered Democrats vote for a Democratic candidate, and registered Republicans vote for a Republican candidate. But some states hold a primary caucus instead of an election and sometimes the results do not bear resemblance to the wishes of the majority of people.

In seventeen states there is an open primary where any registered voter can vote. For example, in Alabama or Georgia, a registered Democrat or Independent can vote in the Republican primary. States use either an open, closed, or semi-closed election for their primaries.

In the final election, however, people can vote for whichever candidate they like, regardless of their party. They may even choose to cast what is called a *mixed ticket*—selecting candidates from different parties for various offices. Voters also have the right not to vote for any of the people whose names are printed

| 1-L | OFFICIAL BALLOT, GENERAL ELECTION PALM BEACH COUNTY, FLORIDA NOVEMBER 7, 2000 | | OFFICIAL BALLOT, GENERAL ELECTION PALM BEACH COUNTY, FLORIDA NOVEMBER 7, 2000 | 1-R |

	(REPUBLICAN) GEORGE W. BUSH - PRESIDENT DICK CHENEY - VICE PRESIDENT	3 ▶
	(DEMOCRATIC) AL GORE - PRESIDENT JOE LIEBERMAN - VICE PRESIDENT	5 ▶
ELECTORS FOR PRESIDENT AND VICE PRESIDENT (A vote for the candidates will actually be a vote for their electors.) (Vote for Group)	(LIBERTARIAN) HARRY BROWNE - PRESIDENT ART OLIVIER - VICE PRESIDENT	7 ▶
	(GREEN) RALPH NADER - PRESIDENT WINONA LaDUKE - VICE PRESIDENT	9 ▶
	(SOCIALIST WORKER) JAMES HARRIS - PRESIDENT MARGARET TROWE - VICE PRESIDENT	11 ▶
	(NATURAL LAW) JOHN HAGELIN - PRESIDENT NAT GOLDHABER VICE PRESIDENT	13 ▶

◀ 4	(REFORM) PAT BUCHANAN - PRESIDENT EZOLA FOSTER - VICE PRESIDENT
◀ 6	(SOCIALIST) DAVID McREYNOLDS - PRESIDENT MARY CAL HOLLIS - VICE PRESIDENT
◀ 8	(CONSTITUTION) HOWARD PHILLIPS - PRESIDENT J. CURTIS FRAZIER - VICE PRESIDENT
◀ 10	(WORKERS WORLD) MONICA MOOREHEAD - PRESIDENT GLORIA La RIVA - VICE PRESIDENT

WRITE-IN CANDIDATE
To vote for a write-in candidate, follow the directions on the long stub of your ballot card.

In 2000, candidates from ten political parties were nominated for U.S. president. Voters could also write in a candidate if they did not want to vote for any of the others.

on the ballot. Instead, they may write the name of the person they want to win on a separate line. The person they choose is called a *write-in candidate.*

In recent years many states have leaned either Democratic or Republican. For years, several states have had governors and representatives from both houses of Congress that belong to the same party. In this way many people think our two-party system is more like a one-party system. Some people think that the two-party system works poorly. They point out that many Democrats and Republicans put more effort into arguing with each other than into solving the nation's problems.

Independents can be broken down into several specialized groups. The term *third party* is often used to describe a candidate

Ralph Nader (left), a presidential candidate in 1996 and 2000, helped spread the ideas and popularity of the Green Party. In 1992, thousands of people voted for him as a write-in candidate.

OCTOBER 18 – NOVEMBER 1, 2010 ■ www.TeaPartyExpress.org

TEA PARTY EXPRESS IV

LIBERTY AT THE BALLOT BOX

Tea Party supporters rallied hard in 2010 to get more conservative representatives into Congress. Their success led many to believe they would nominate a candidate for president in 2012.

from one of these groups. Two of the most popular are the Green Party and the more recently formed Tea Party. Members of the Green Party think the environment should be a top concern in most political decisions. Tea party members think the nation should get back to its earliest roots. They think that taxes have gotten out of control again, like they were in the days of the Boston Tea Party.

The term *Tea Party* is a bit of a play on words. It refers to the historical event we call the Boston Tea Party. When this event occurred, tea was a heavily taxed import. Some people say that the tea in our modern Tea Party stands for taxed enough already.

Does Every Vote Make a Difference?

In 1984, the Democratic Party made history. Walter Mondale, the former vice president under Jimmy Carter, had chosen Geraldine Ferraro as his running mate. It was the first time a woman played a key role in the race for the White House.

At the Democratic convention, Ferraro told the excited crowd, "As I stand before the American people and think of the honor this great convention has bestowed upon me, I recall the words of Dr. Martin Luther King Jr., who made America stronger by making America more free. He said, 'Occasionally in life there are moments that cannot be completely explained by words. Their meaning can only be articulated by the inaudible language of the heart.' Tonight is such a moment for me. My heart is filled with pride. My fellow citizens, I proudly accept your nomination for vice president of the United States."[1]

Mondale and Ferraro had a tough race ahead of them. They were up against Ronald Reagan and George H. W. Bush, who had already served one term in the White House. That November, Mondale and Ferraro lost the election to Reagan and Bush, but millions of

Walter Mondale (left) claps as Geraldine Ferraro speaks to a crowd during their 1984 presidential campaign.

Americans saw the race as a huge win in the battle for gender equality.

National elections have a great impact on our nation. These races are held every two years. They determine who will represent each state in both houses of Congress. Sometimes they also decide who the country's president and vice president will be.

The people of the United States elect a president every four years. If the current president has served only one term, he or she may choose to run one more time. A sitting politician who runs for another term is called the incumbent. Most incumbents win the nomination of their parties, because they are already well known. A president who has already served two terms is called a lame duck. This expression means that the president no longer has the power to implement his policies. Politicians who are still in office after other candidates have won their seats are also called lame ducks for this reason.

The number of congressmen or congresswomen a state has depends on its population. Larger states, like California and Texas, have the most. Geographic area has no effect on the number. The relatively small state of New York has 29 representatives, but the huge state of Alaska has just 1. Currently, there are 435 members of Congress who are elected every two years. Geographic location does play a part in making up districts. These areas determine which representative votes for you in Congress. Politicians must be legal residents of their districts, usually for at least one to five years, depending on the job.[2]

There is no limit to the number of times members of Congress can be reelected. Oftentimes younger politicians begin their careers as representatives. After a few terms in Congress, they run for Senate seats. Because of this, one might call the House of Representatives a common stepping stone to the Senate.

Each state has two senators, regardless of the state's size or population. Therefore, the Senate has a total of 100 members.

Every state has two senate districts. Senators are elected every six years. Not all Senate seats are up for reelection at the same time, however. Every two years one-third of the senators must decide whether they want to run again. Like members of the House of Representatives, senators can run for reelection as many times as they like.

Some people think that there should be term limits for Congress and the Senate just as there is a term limit for the presidency. These people think that it is best to keep putting new politicians in office every few years. Some senators have held their offices for decades. Their long-term service has made many of them very powerful and popular—and made it more difficult for new people to get elected.

Presidential election years can be very exciting. In those years, a national convention is held. Thousands of people attend in person, and millions more watch on television. Both the Democratic and the Republican conventions are held every four years, a few months before the presidential election. Conventions usually last about five days. During this time the candidates and other party members give speeches. The candidate with the most electoral votes becomes the nominee for that party. He or she also chooses a running mate around this time. This is the person who will become the vice president if the presidential candidate wins the race.

A running mate may be one of the other original candidates or another person entirely. It must be someone from the same party, though. Many times a candidate will select a running mate that complements his or her strengths and weaknesses. For instance, a

VOTE

Election Day is always the first Tuesday following the first Monday in November. If November 1 falls on a Monday, Election Day will be November 2. If November 1 falls on a Tuesday, Election Day will be November 8.

younger candidate with less political experience may choose an older running mate who has been a senator for numerous years. Likewise, a candidate who is thought to be weak on foreign policy might select a running mate who has worked as an ambassador to an overseas country. Candidates usually choose running mates who are likely to attract a high number of votes. These decisions are all part of campaign strategy.

Election years can be a little overwhelming. Television and radio stations—even street corners and vehicle bumpers—are flooded with advertisements for the candidates. Many politicians run clean campaigns. This means that they use their ads to talk about the issues instead of their opponents' flaws. Some people who run for public office resort to mudslinging. They try to make their opponents look bad by bringing up embarrassing mistakes they have made.

You may assume that the citizens of the United States—the voters—decide who will be president. This is only partly accurate. The winner isn't always the candidate who wins the most votes (popular vote). Instead, the electors from the Electoral College decide how many electoral votes each candidate receives based on the popular vote. The Electoral College casts their votes about a month after the national election. Congress does not formally count them until the beginning of January.[3]

There are a total of 538 electoral votes. Each state has a specific number of votes assigned to it. The exact number is based on the state's population. A candidate must receive 270 electoral votes to win the presidency. Technically, it is possible for no one

A presidential candidate must receive the majority of electoral votes to win the office. If no candidate receives more than 50 percent of the electoral votes, the House of Representatives chooses the winner. Two former presidents have been selected this way: Thomas Jefferson and John Quincy Adams.

US Elections 2000

The presidential election of 2000 offers an example of how the Electoral College affects the presidency. The map shows how many electoral votes each state had that year. The person who won the most electoral votes (and therefore the election) was George W. Bush, but the winner of the popular vote was Al Gore.

to receive enough electoral votes to win the presidential election. In this event the House of Representatives selects the president.

Although the Electoral College has been in place for centuries, many people think that it is a poor way of selecting a president. Many citizens feel their votes do not count because of the electoral system. Others think that the system works well and should remain in place.

Close to Home

Barack Obama's 2008 presidential victory has paved the way for many other African-American candidates to succeed in politics. It is important to remember, though, that many local candidates helped to pave the way for President Obama. In 1990, Lawrence Douglas Wilder from Virginia was one of them.

The grandson of slaves, Wilder had grown up in a segregated community in Richmond. He went on to earn a master's degree in chemistry, but his career path took a sharp turn in 1954. The Supreme Court had just ruled in the case of *Brown v. Board of Education of Topeka, Kansas*. The decision brought segregation to an end. Inspired by this important ruling, Wilder decided to enter law school—and eventually to enter local politics.

He didn't become governor overnight. He started out by running as a Democrat for the Virginia state senate in 1969. He won this race against two white candidates. Next he ran for the position of lieutenant governor.[1] Not every state has this position. A lieutenant governor is similar to a vice president in some ways. The lieutenant governor is first in line to take over the governor's position should he or she become

Lawrence Douglas Wilder became the first African-American governor of Virginia. In 1991, he announced he would run for president.

Three U.S. presidents began their political careers as mayors. Grover Cleveland was mayor of Buffalo, New York. Calvin Coolidge served as mayor of Northampton, Massachusetts. Andrew Johnson was mayor of Greeneville, Tennessee.

unable to serve. Unlike a vice president and president, though, a lieutenant governor and governor are elected separately.

After four years as lieutenant governor, Wilder ran for governor of Virginia. It was the closest governor's race the state had seen in the entire twentieth century. When the recount was done, Wilder had won by only 6,741 votes out of more than 1.7 million, but this small difference was enough to make him the first African-American elected governor in the nation.[2]

Like the presidency and other national offices, local government also depends on the voters to select its representatives. Local elections include races for governor, state representatives, mayor, and city council. Some areas also elect sheriffs, city clerks, and school board members. Many politicians begin working at this grassroots level and slowly work their way into higher offices. Numerous presidents of the United States have been former state governors. A few even started out as mayors.

The blueprint for our federal government is the U.S. Constitution. Every state also has its own constitution. Each of these important documents outlines all the laws for that state. State legislatures work much like the U.S. Congress and Senate to create and pass new laws. Do you know whether it is illegal in your state to drive while talking on a cell phone? What is the minimum age to get a driver's license there? How old must someone be to get a part-time job? These matters are all decided by state legislatures.

Some laws that have been on the books for decades in certain states can be quite humorous. For example, in Maine it is against the law to keep Christmas decorations up after January 14. In

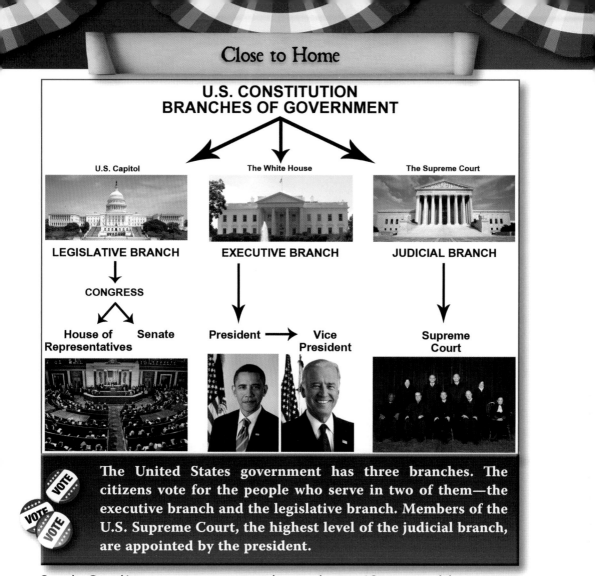

U.S. CONSTITUTION
BRANCHES OF GOVERNMENT

U.S. Capitol — The White House — The Supreme Court

LEGISLATIVE BRANCH — EXECUTIVE BRANCH — JUDICIAL BRANCH

CONGRESS

House of Representatives — Senate — President → Vice President — Supreme Court

The United States government has three branches. The citizens vote for the people who serve in two of them—the executive branch and the legislative branch. Members of the U.S. Supreme Court, the highest level of the judicial branch, are appointed by the president.

South Carolina, a person must be at least 18 years old to use a pinball machine. Missouri state law has made it illegal to drive with an uncaged bear in the vehicle.[3]

The more serious side of local politics can be extremely interesting. Some cities broadcast their city council meetings on local television stations. Community members can watch from home or attend an event to speak in front of the council about a particular issue. It is a council member's job to vote on issues that affect the community. The community members do not get to vote on most issues themselves. They do, however, vote for the councilors who represent them.

Name	Position	Party	Took office	Up for reelection
Kwame R. Brown	Chairman	Democratic	2007	2014
Michael A. Brown	At-large	Independent	2009	2012
David Catania	At-large	Independent	1997	2014
Phil Mendelson	At-large	Democratic	1999	2014
Vincent Orange	At-large	Democratic	2011	2012
Jim Graham	Ward 1	Democratic	1999	2014
Jack Evans	Ward 2	Democratic	1991	2012
Mary Cheh	Ward 3	Democratic	2007	2014
Muriel Bowser	Ward 4	Democratic	2007	2012
vacant	Ward 5	N/A	N/A	N/A
Tommy Wells	Ward 6	Democratic	2007	2014
Yvette Alexander	Ward 7	Democratic	2007	2012
Marion Barry	Ward 8	Democratic	2005	2012

The District of Columbia has its own city council. Each of the area's eight districts has its own representative. There are also five at-large members who represent everyone who lives in Washington, D.C. However, except for three votes in the Electoral College, its residents do not have representation at the federal level.

The terms of most local offices vary from one area to another. City councilors usually serve two-year terms. Serving in local government is a big job that rarely comes with many benefits. In many areas the only city-level politician who gets paid is the mayor. Many local politicians volunteer their time to these positions to make their communities better places.

Most governors serve for four years at a time. Exceptions are the governors of New Hampshire and Vermont. Both of these states elect new governors every two years instead. Most state representatives serve two-year terms. Term limits are also a concern at the local level. Some people have held offices in their state legislatures for as long as some U.S. senators have held on to their seats.

Most states allow their governors to serve up to two consecutive terms. A governor may, however, choose to run for reelection after taking a term off. Interestingly, neither New Hampshire nor Vermont imposes a term limit on this office.

When local decisions cause excessive debate, an issue may turn into a referendum question for voters. People on both sides of the issue may gather signatures from voters. If enough citizens sign one of these petitions, the issue is then placed on the ballot at the next election. Common referendum questions include whether to spend large amounts of money on education, building or repairing bridges and roads, and the addition of businesses such as casinos. Referendum questions may also relate to putting limits on new taxes.

Sometimes special elections are held when a specific need arises. If a representative quits or passes away, the position must be refilled. In some cases the other members vote to fill the vacancy. Other times the people must vote for the replacement. It all depends on the city or state. Unlike the president, a mayor doesn't have a person in line to take over in this type of situation.

Whether people are voting in a national election or a local one, they will cast their ballot close to home. The exact location depends on where they live. All cities and towns are divided into districts, similar to the way the state is divided into congressional and senatorial districts. When a family has more than one home, they must select one to be their legal residence. This is where the adults will vote. Many districts vote in the gymnasiums of local schools. Others vote at community centers. A few even vote at nearby fire halls. Citizens can find out where they should go to vote by calling their local city offices.

Not only do the people vote politicians into office, but they also pay their salaries. The salaries of national representatives come from federal tax money. City and state representatives are paid from local tax dollars.

Chapter 5

What You Can Do for Your Country

You probably haven't heard of Westbrook, Maine. This suburb isn't as well known as its neighboring city of Portland. Likewise, you probably haven't heard of Michael Foley. He isn't as well known as the other politicians in this book, at least not yet. In 2005, Foley was doing what many other 18-year-olds were doing. He was getting ready to graduate from high school and deciding where he would go to college. Unlike most other high school seniors, though, Foley was also running for city council.

The race quickly became a hot topic among local voters. Could this young Democratic candidate handle the demanding position of a council member while still in school? After all, he still had homework to do every night. He also had no practical experience. What he did have was a new outlook that voters found refreshing. He could relate to the younger people in the community, but he was also remarkably mature. It was starting to look like he had a fighting chance. When November rolled around, the voters of Westbrook made it official. Foley became one of the youngest city council members in the nation.

Michael Foley became an elected politician while he was still in high school.

Surprisingly, Foley began his political career even before the citywide election. Before running for city council, he served as a student representative on the Westbrook School Committee. He seemed to know from a very early age that young people can contribute a lot to local government.[1]

Some schools hold mock elections at the same time real elections are taking place. Exercises like these can be a great way for young people to learn about the voting process. An astonishing number of these pretend races have the same outcome as the real things, sometimes even days before the actual elections. One reason may be that many kids vote for the same candidates they know their parents will be voting for.

Many schools also offer students a chance to participate in student governments of their own. Students can run for positions on their school's student council. They campaign just like real politicians. They make speeches about the issues, ask for other students' votes, and create fun buttons and posters.

The students who become class representatives work together with teachers and principals to mold school policies. They also plan events. Student councils often sponsor fundraising activities such as carnivals, dances, and bake sales. Some student governments even create volunteer opportunities for kids through local nursing homes, soup kitchens, and animal shelters.

Many young people can hardly wait to be old enough to vote in a real election. They want to get involved in the process now. Just because they cannot cast ballots yet doesn't mean they can't volunteer their time to a local political campaign. They can help a certain candidate get elected by stuffing envelopes, putting up signs, or delivering flyers about his or her platform.

The Twenty-sixth Amendment lowered the voting age from 21 to 18. Some people think that it should be lowered again, perhaps to 16.

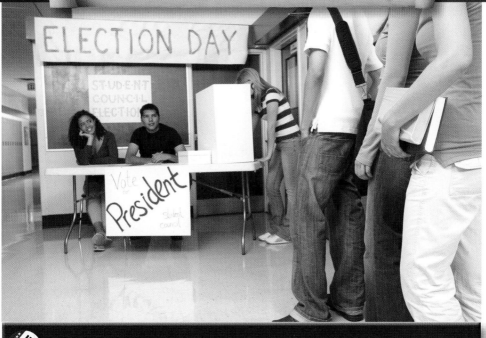

School elections help introduce the concept of voting to young people. Kids may not be able to make all the decisions about their schools and education, but they can have some say in these matters by getting involved in student government.

Working on a political campaign can be a great opportunity. Every vote makes a difference, but helping a favorite candidate receive as many votes as possible makes an even greater one. Before they know it, young volunteers will be ready to become registered voters themselves.

In the past, the polls showed that most young people (between the ages of 18 and 29) were not voting. Candidates focused on the older adults who were voting instead. Today young people make up a huge part of the voting public. In the year 2000, about 15 million people aged 18 to 29 voted. By 2004 this number had increased to more than 20 million. In 2008 the number grew yet again. In some states the number of voters had doubled or even tripled from 2004.[2]

A nonprofit organization called Rock the Vote encourages young people to get involved in the voting process. It uses popular music,

Musicians—like Snoop Dogg and other members of 213—helped spread the word about the importance of voting through the Rock the Vote Bus Tour.

celebrities, and the latest technology to help young people understand how important voting is. More than 5 million young people have registered to vote through this group, and the numbers just keep increasing. The group also urges young adults to work together to fight unfair voter registration practices.[3]

In some states citizens can register to vote on the same day as an election. In other states, same-day registration is not allowed. Critics of same-day registration worry that mistakes will be made if registration is made too easy and quick. Some believe that rules will be broken on purpose. Another issue that is sometimes debated is whether voters should have to show identification before voting. In some places showing ID is required, while in others it is not necessary.

Another commonly debated topic is whether the voting age should be lowered. Most people are considered adults when they reach the age of 18. Some people think that 16-year-olds are old enough to be able to make sensible voting decisions, however. Those in favor of lowering the voting age argue that getting young people involved in the voting process earlier will help to keep them interested in politics. Others worry that these teenagers are still too influenced by their parents and peers to form opinions that are truly their own.

Many different groups spend a great deal of time and money gathering information from voters. One of the most important questions they ask when polling voters is for whom they plan to vote. This data can be extremely helpful throughout a campaign. If voters from a certain area are planning to vote for someone, that person's opponent knows that stumping there will be especially important. Polls can also inspire voters to get involved. If a

 Students at San Diego University register to vote. Young voters can make a big difference in national elections. Even people who are too young to vote can start petitions that will bring about big changes in businesses and government.

Voting booths can look very different depending on where they are located. Some states give voters pens and paper ballots. Others provide cards and punch tools for marking votes. Some states even use computers for voting.

candidate isn't doing very well in the polls, his or her supporters may decide to volunteer to help the campaign. At the same time, polls can also discourage some voters. In some cases it even causes them to consider changing their votes.

★ ★ ★ ★ ★ ★ ★ ★ ★ ★ ★ ★ ★

Early
Voting Here

Votación
Anticipada Aquí

★ ★ ★ ★ ★ ★ ★ ★ ★ ★ ★ ★ ★

Polls that are taken immediately after voters have left the voting booths are called exit polls. Even though the people answering the questions have already voted, exit polls can have a big effect on elections. People who have not voted yet may decide not to bother voting after hearing the results. They may feel they do not want to waste their time voting for a candidate who is probably going to lose. But what could happen if everyone who felt this way did vote? Other people might assume that a candidate who is currently in the lead doesn't need just one more vote. Many leading candidates have lost their leads—and even the elections—for this reason.

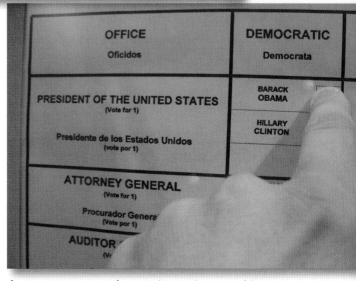

OFFICE Oficidos	DEMOCRATIC Democrata
PRESIDENT OF THE UNITED STATES (Vote for 1) Presidente de los Estados Unidos (vote por 1)	BARACK OBAMA HILLARY CLINTON
ATTORNEY GENERAL (Vote for 1) Procurador Genera (Vote por 1)	
AUDITOR	

A voter uses an electronic voting machine to choose a Democratic candidate in a primary election.

Not everyone makes it to the polls on Election Day. Campaign volunteers help some people by giving them rides, but others still cannot get there. They may be in the hospital, on vacation, or serving in the military. If people know beforehand that they won't be able to vote in person, they can fill out an absentee ballot.[4] That way they don't lose their chance to be heard.

Voting is one of the most precious rights Americans have. Choosing not to use it is like giving up a little piece of freedom. When you reach voting age, you may realize that another excellent way of making a difference is getting involved on the other side of an election. Deciding which issues matter most to you may inspire you to run for public office one day. If you see something you don't like in the world, do what you can to change it.

"Bad politicians are sent to Washington by good people who don't vote."—William E. Simon (businessman, philanthropist, and 63rd United States Secretary of the Treasury)

1773	The Boston Tea Party takes place.
1783	The American colonists win the Revolutionary War against England.
1788	The U.S. Constitution is ratified.
1790	Only white men who own property are allowed to vote.
1792	Thomas Jefferson and James Madison start the Democratic Party.
1848	The first women's rights convention takes place in Seneca Falls, New York.
1850	Voters are no longer required to own property, but still only white men can vote.
1854	The Republican Party is formed.
1855	The first literacy tests for voting are used in Connecticut. Their purpose is to keep Irish-Catholic citizens from voting.
1857	Massachusetts begins using a similar literacy test to Connecticut's.
1865	The Union wins the Civil War against the Confederate States of America.
1870	The Fifteenth Amendment passes. It grants all male citizens, regardless of race, the right to vote.
1872	Susan B. Anthony and thirteen other women vote in an election in Rochester, New York.
1889	Florida begins charging voters a poll tax. Because many African-American men are poor, this keeps them from voting. Ten other Southern states follow Florida's lead in dodging the Fifteenth Amendment.
1890	Mississippi begins using literacy tests for voting. Their purpose is to keep African Americans from voting.
1913	The Seventeenth Amendment passes. U.S. senators are now elected by the people instead of by state legislatures.
1920	The Nineteenth Amendment passes. It grants women the right to vote.
1924	The Indian Citizenship Act passes. It grants Native Americans citizenship, which allows them to vote under the Fifteenth Amendment.
1964	The Twenty-fourth Amendment passes. It makes poll taxes illegal.
1965	The Voting Rights Act passes. It makes literacy tests illegal.
1971	The Twenty-sixth Amendment lowers the minimum voting age to 18.
1984	Walter Mondale selects Geraldine Ferraro as his running mate for the presidential election, making her the first female candidate for vice president.
1990	Lawrence Douglass Wilder becomes the first African American elected governor in the United States.
1996	The Green Party is formed, with a focus on the environment.
1999	The Tea Party Movement begins holding local protests.
2000	Vice President Al Gore wins the popular vote for the U.S. presidency; Texas Governor George W. Bush wins the electoral vote, and therefore becomes the 43rd U.S. president.

2008 Barack Obama becomes the first African-American president of the United States.

2010 Republicans experience sweeping victories in midterm congressional elections. They take the majority in the House of Representatives with a total of 242 seats.

2011 A new law in Florida leads the League of Women Voters to suspend new registration drives in the state. The group has been helping women register to vote for 72 years, but the threat of fines gets in the way. The league would have to pay between $50 and $1,000 for each voter they register if paperwork is not returned to election officials by a certain time.

2012 In January, campaigning has already begun for the November election.

Chapter Notes

Chapter 1. The Right to Vote
1. Boston Tea Party Historical Society, "The Destruction of Tea in Numbers and Facts," http://www.boston-tea-party.org/facts-numbers.html
2. Susan B. Anthony Center for Women's Leadership, "Women's Rights Convention in Seneca Falls, NY," http://www.rochester.edu/sba/suffragewomensrights.html
3. PBS, "RACE: The Power of an Illusion," http://www.pbs.org/race/000_About/002_03_d-godeeper.htm

Chapter 2. The Life of the Party
1. Chris Cillizza, "Specter to Switch Parties," *The Washington Post,* April 28, 2009, http://voices.washingtonpost.com/thefix/senate/specter-to-switch-parties.html
2. Declare Yourself, "State By State Info," http://www.declareyourself.com/voting_faq/state_by_state_info_2.html

Chapter 3. Does Every Vote Make a Difference?
1. CNN AllPolitics: "Ferraro's Acceptance Speech, 1984," http://www.cnn.com/ALLPOLITICS/1996/conventions/chicago/facts/famous.speeches/ferraro.84.shtml
2. United States House of Representatives: "The House Explained," http://www.house.gov/content/learn/
3. U.S. Electoral College, "Summary of Key Dates, Events & Information," http://www.archives.gov/federal-register/electoral-college/2008/dates.html

Chapter 4. Close to Home

1. Virginia Historical Society: "L. Douglas Wilder." http://www.vahistorical. org/sva2003/wilder.htm
2. Art Pine, "First Elected Black Governor Takes His Oath," *Los Angeles Times,* January 14, 1990, http://articles.latimes.com/1990-01-14/news/ mn-271_1_elected-black-governor
3. *The Huffington Post,* "17 Ridiculous Laws Still on the Books in the U.S.," March 2, 2010, http://www.huffingtonpost.com/2010/03/02/ 17-ridiculous-laws-still_n_481379.html#s71645&title=In_Missouri_It

Chapter 5. What You Can Do for Your Country

1. Elbert Aull, "Westbrook Seeks Ways to Cultivate Teen Input," *Portland Press Herald,* January 28, 2009; online at Maine Youth Action Network, http://www.myan.org/?more_maine_stories
2. Young Democrats of America, "Youth Voting Stats," http://www.yda.org/ resources/youth-vote-statistics/
3. Rock the Vote, http://www.rockthevote.org/
4. Federal Voting Assistance Program, "Find Your State," http://www.fvap.gov/map.html

Further Reading

Books

Colman, Penny. *Elizabeth Cady Stanton and Susan B. Anthony—A Friendship That Changed the World.* New York: Henry Holt & Company, 2011.

Lankford, Ronnie D. *Should the Voting Age Be Lowered?* Farmington Hills, Michigan: Greenhaven Press, 2008.

Miller, David. *Vote.* New York: DK Publishing, 2008.

Works Consulted

Boston Tea Party Historical Society. http://www.boston-tea-party.org/index. html

Brennan, Jason F. *The Ethics of Voting.* Princeton, New Jersey: Princeton University Press, 2011.

Bullock, Charles S., III, and Ronald Keith Gaddie. *The Triumph of Voting Rights in the South.* Norman: University of Oklahoma Press, 2009.

Burnham, Walter Dean. *Voting in American Elections.* Palo Alto, California: Academica Press, 2009.

Cillizza, Chris. "Specter to Switch Parties." *The Washington Post,* April 28, 2009. http://voices.washingtonpost.com/thefix/senate/specter-to-switch-parties.html

CNN AllPolitics: "Ferraro's Acceptance Speech, 1984." http://www.cnn.com/ALLPOLITICS/1996/conventions/chicago/facts/famous.speeches/ferraro.84.shtml

Dahl, Melissa. "Youth Vote May Have Been Key in Obama's Win." *MSNBC,* November 5, 2008. http://www.msnbc.msn.com/id/27525497/ns/politics-decision_08/t/youth-vote-may-have-been-key-obamas-win/

Federal Voting Assistance Program. http://www.fvap.gov

The Huffington Post. "17 Ridiculous Laws Still on the Books in the U.S." March 2, 2010. http://www.huffingtonpost.com/2010/03/02/17-ridiculous-laws-still_n_481379.html#s71645&title=In_Missouri_It

Maine Youth Action Network. http://www.myan.org

Pine, Art. "First Elected Black Governor Takes His Oath." *Los Angeles Times,* January 14, 1990. http://articles.latimes.com/1990-01-14/news/mn-271_1_elected-black-governor

United States House of Representatives: "The House Explained." http://www.house.gov/content/learn/

Virginia Historical Society: "L. Douglas Wilder." http://www.vahistorical.org/sva2003/wilder.htm

Wattenberg, Martin P. *Is Voting For Young People?* New York: Longman, 2007.

Young Democrats of America. http://www.yda.org

On the Internet

ACE Electoral Knowledge Network: "Voter Education at Voting Sites" http://aceproject.org/ace-en/topics/ve/vea/vea04/vea04e/vea04e02

Kids Voting USA http://kidsvotingusa.org/

Rock the Vote http://www.rockthevote.org/

The U.S. Electoral College http://www.archives.gov/federal-register/electoral-college/index.html

Vote411.org http://www.vote411.org/

atheist (AY-thee-ist)—A person who does not believe in a higher power, such as God.

caucus (KAW-kus)—A meeting among members of a political party for the purpose of selecting a candidate.

conservative (kun-SER-vah-tiv)—A person who holds traditional political views.

delegate (DEH-leh-git)—A person acting on behalf of another person or group of people.

democracy (deh-MAH-kruh-see)—A form of government in which the majority of voters makes decisions.

Democrat (DEH-muh-krat)—A member of the Democratic party.

district (DIS-trikt)—The area represented by a particular political representative.

Electoral College (ee-LEK-tor-ul KAH-lidj)—The group that tallies the number of electoral votes each candidate wins in a presidential election.

endorse (en-DORS)—To give a specific candidate one's official approval in an election.

felon (FEH-lun)—A person who has committed a serious crime (a felony).

freeholder (FREE-hol-der)—A landowner.

grassroots (GRAS-roots)—The most local level of government.

incumbent (in-KUM-bent)—A political candidate who currently holds an office and is running for re-election.

independent (in-dee-PEN-dent)—A registered voter or political candidate who prefers not to join either the Democratic or Republican party.

lame duck (LAYM DUK)—A current politician who cannot run for re-election or who has lost his or her seat to another candidate.

liberal (LIB-rul)—A person who holds progressive political views.

moderate (MAH-duh-rut)—A person whose political views are neither conservative nor liberal.

nominate (NAH-mih-nayt)—To choose a political candidate.

platform (PLAT-form)—A political candidate's opinions about important matters relating to the people.

popular vote (POP-yoo-lur VOHT)—The votes cast by individual citizens.

primary (PRY-mayr-ee)—An early election for the purpose of choosing a candidate from each political party.

referendum (reh-fer-EN-dum)—A question that is placed on the ballot for local voters.

representative (rep-ree-ZEN-tah-tiv)—A person who is elected to vote for a group of people.

Republican (ree-PUB-lih-kun)—A member of the Republican party.

segregation (seh-greh-GAY-shun)—The separation of people based on race, gender, class, or ethnicity.

suffrage (SUH-fridj)—The right to vote.

Index

absentee ballot 41
Adams, John Quincy 26
African Americans 8, 10–11, 28, 29
amendments 7, 8, 10, 11, 36
Anthony, Susan B. 8, 9, 10
Boston Tea Party 4, 5, 21
Bush, George H. W. 22
Bush, George W. 27
campaign strategy 26
caucuses 25
city councils 31–32, 34
civil rights era 11
Civil War 8
Cleveland, Grover 30
Coolidge, Calvin 30
delegates 25
democracy 6
Democrats 12, 13, 14, 17–20, 22, 25, 28, 34
districts 24, 32–33
Election Day 14, 16, 25, 41
Electoral College 26–27, 32, 34
exit polls 39–41
felons 14
Ferraro, Geraldine 22, 23
Foley, Michael 34, 35, 36
Franklin, Benjamin 7, 8
freeholders 6–7, 8
Gore, Al 27
Green Party 20–21, 30
incumbents 24
independents 18–21, 32
Jefferson, Thomas 26
Johnson, Andrew 30
lame ducks 24
literacy tests 10, 11
moderates 17
Mondale, Walter 22, 23
Nader, Ralph 20

National Woman Suffrage Association 8
Native Americans 11
Obama, Barack 28
petitions 33, 39
political parties 17
poll taxes 10, 11
popular vote 26–27
primaries 19, 25, 41
Reagan, Ronald 22
referendum questions 33
religious discrimination 7, 8
Republicans 12, 13, 14, 17–20, 25
Revolutionary War 6
Rock the Vote 37–38
running mate 22, 25–26
Simon, William E. 41
special elections 33
Specter, Arlen 12, 13
Stanton, Elizabeth Cady 8, 9
student government 36, 37
Tea Party 20–21
term limits 25, 32–33
U.S. Constitution 6, 17, 30, 31
U.S. House of Representatives (Congress) 18, 20, 24–27, 30, 31
U.S. Senate 12, 24–25, 30, 31
volunteering 14, 17, 32, 36–37, 40–41
voter registration 14, 15, 16, 18–19, 37–38
voting age 36, 38–39, 41
Washington, D.C. 7, 32
Wilder, Lawrence Douglas 28, 29, 30
women's suffrage 7, 8, 9, 10–11
write-in candidates 19

Tammy Gagne is the author of numerous books for adults and children, including *My Guide to the Constitution: The Power of the States* and *What It's Like to Be Sonia Sotomayor* for Mitchell Lane Publishers. She considers voting to be one of the most important responsibilities that Americans have. She resides in northern New England with her husband and son. One of her favorite pastimes is visiting schools to speak to kids about the writing process.